Indiana

By Judith Jensen Hyde

Subject Consultant
Nancy Wolfe
Educational Consultant and Writer
Indianapolis, Indiana

Reading Consultant
Cecilia Minden-Cupp, PhD
Former Director of the Language and Literacy Program
Harvard Graduate School of Education
Cambridge, Massachusetts

Children's Press®
A Division of Scholastic Inc.
New York   Toronto   London   Auckland   Sydney
Mexico City   New Delhi   Hong Kong
Danbury, Connecticut

Designer: Herman Adler
Photo Researcher: Caroline Anderson
The photo on the cover shows an Indiana farm.

Library of Congress Cataloging-in-Publication Data

Hyde, Judith Jensen, 1947-
    Indiana / by Judith Jensen Hyde.
        p. cm. — (Rookie read-about geography)
    Includes index.
    ISBN-13: 978-0-516-21846-5 (lib. bdg.)   978-0-516-21618-8 (pbk.)
    ISBN-10: 0-516-21846-8 (lib. bdg.)   0-516-21618-X (pbk.)
    1. Indiana—Juvenile literature. 2. Indiana—Geography—Juvenile
    literature. I. Title. II. Series.
    F526.3.H94 2006
    977.2—dc22   2006004585

CHILDREN'S PRESS, and ROOKIE READ-ABOUT®, and associated
logos are trademarks and/or registered trademarks of Scholastic Library
Publishing. SCHOLASTIC and associated logos are trademarks and/or
registered trademarks of Scholastic Inc.
1 2 3 4 5 6 7 8 9 10 R 16 15 14 13 12 11 10 09 08 07

Which state has beaches, underground caves, and car races? It's Indiana!

Visitors enjoy Lake Michigan at an Indiana beach.

Indiana is in the midwestern part of the United States. It touches Illinois, Kentucky, Michigan, and Ohio.

Can you find Indiana on this map?

CANADA

WASHINGTON
MONTANA
NORTH DAKOTA
MINNESOTA
NEW HAMPSHIRE
VERMONT
MAINE

OREGON
IDAHO
SOUTH DAKOTA
WISCONSIN
MICHIGAN
NEW YORK
MASSACHUSETTS
RHODE ISLAND

WYOMING
IOWA
PENNSYLVANIA
CONNECTICUT
NEW JERSEY

NEVADA
UTAH
NEBRASKA
ILLINOIS
INDIANA
OHIO
WEST VIRGINIA
DELAWARE
MARYLAND

COLORADO
KANSAS
MISSOURI
KENTUCKY
VIRGINIA
Washington, D.C.

CALIFORNIA
ARIZONA
NEW MEXICO
OKLAHOMA
ARKANSAS
TENNESSEE
NORTH CAROLINA

TEXAS
MISSISSIPPI
ALABAMA
GEORGIA
SOUTH CAROLINA

LOUISIANA
FLORIDA

North
West East
South

ALASKA
CANADA
MEXICO
HAWAII

A farm on Indiana's Till Plains

Indiana has three main
land sections, or regions.
These regions are called
the Great Lakes Plains,
the Till Plains, and
the Southern Plains
and Lowlands.

Grass grows on the sand dunes at Indiana Dunes National Lakeshore.

10

Indiana Dunes National Lakeshore is located along Lake Michigan. This spot is famous for its sand dunes.

Sand dunes are hills of sand that are shaped by wind. They are usually found along a beach.

The Till Plains are in central Indiana. Long ago, large, moving blocks of ice called glaciers could be found there.

The glaciers left behind a mixture of sand, clay, and rock. This mixture is called till.

A field in the Till Plains

An Indiana corn farm

The soil in the Till Plains is perfect for farming.

Farmers there grow soybeans, tomatoes, and corn. Others raise cows, chickens, and hogs.

The Southern Plains and Lowlands make up the hilliest part of the state. This region is filled with many steep hills called knobs.

Knobs in the Southern Plains

If you visit Indiana, you can explore many caves.

Underground streams in this region have created many mysterious caves.

Miners dig for coal and limestone in the Southern Plains and Lowlands. Limestone is a rock that is used for building.

Indiana is home to many animals, including bats, deer, and foxes.

The state bird is the cardinal.

A cardinal

A peony

Indiana's state flower is the peony (PEE-yuh-nee). The state tree is the tulip tree.

Indiana has many rivers.
The Ohio River runs along
Indiana's southern border.

The Wabash River is in
the north. It is Indiana's
state river.

A bridge over Indiana's Wabash River

Lake
Michigan

MICHIGAN

Indiana Dunes
National Seashore

Great Lake
Plains

North
West · East
South

OHIO

INDIANA

ILLINOIS

⊕ Indianapolis

Till Plains

Wabash River

Southern Plains
and Lowlands

KENTUCKY

SCALE 1 inch = 50 miles

0   Miles   50

0   Kilometers   80

Ohio River

26

Indianapolis is the state capital and the largest city in Indiana.

The Indianapolis 500 is an auto race that is held there every year.

Visitors to Indiana can swim and fish. They can climb hills and explore caves.

Would you like to visit Indiana some day? What will you do first?

Visitors to Indiana enjoy a race down a sand dune.

Words You Know

cardinal

cave

corn

knobs

Lake Michigan

peony

sand dunes

Wabash River

31

Index

About the Author

For the past several years, Judith Jensen Hyde has worked as a graphic artist and as a television technician for a large school district in the Kansas City area. Judith and her husband have one grown daughter, one dog, one cat, and one grand-cat.

Photo Credits